P9-DZP-217

Nature's Cycles

FROM Kernel TO Corn

ROBIN NELSON

LERNER PUBLICATIONS COMPANY ▸ Minneapolis

Photo Acknowledgments
The images in this book are used with the permission of:
© D. Normark/PhotoLink/Photodisc/Getty Images, p. 1;
© iStockphoto.com/ronen, p. 3; Courtesy John Deere &
Company, pp. 5, 15; © IndexStock/SuperStock, p. 7;
© Jerome Wexler/Visuals Unlimited, Inc., p. 9; © Suzanne
Tucker/Shutterstock Images, p. 11; © Ed Bock/CORBIS,
p. 13; © Weldon Schloneger/Shutterstock Images, p. 17;
© Jeff and Meggan Haller/CORBIS, p. 19; Bill Tarpenning/
USDA Photo, p. 21; © Todd Strand/Independent Picture
Service, p. 23.

Front cover: © Michelle Meiklejohn/Dreamstime.com.

Lerner Publications Company
A division of Lerner Publishing Group, Inc.
241 First Avenue North
Minneapolis, MN 55401 U.S.A.

Website address: www.lernerbooks.com

Main body text set in Arta Std Book 20/26.
Typeface provided by International Typeface Corp.

Library of Congress Cataloging-in-Publication Data

Nelson, Robin, 1971–
        From kernel to corn / by Robin Nelson.
            p.   cm. — (Start to finish, second series. Nature's
        cycles)
        Includes index.
        ISBN 978–0–7613–8673–5 (lib. bdg. : alk. paper)
        1. Corn—Juvenile literature. I. Title.
SB191.M2N364 2012
633.1'5—dc23   2011024569

Manufactured in the United States of America
1 – DP – 12/31/11

TABLE OF Contents

Corn **tastes yummy!** How does it grow?

3

A farmer prepares for planting.

A farmer drives over a field with a cultivator. This machine has many blades that turn over the dirt. The blades break up clumps of dirt. Now the field is ready for planting.

The farmer plants seeds.

A corn seed is called a **kernel**. The farmer uses a row planter to plant kernels. A row planter is a machine that digs ditches in the field. The row planter puts the kernels in the ditches and covers them with dirt.

The seeds change.

Water helps seeds grow into plants. The kernels soak up water from the dirt. The kernels swell. A **root** breaks open each kernel. Roots grow down into the ground. They take in water and food from the dirt.

9

Tiny plants grow.

Sprouts come out of the kernels. A sprout is a young corn plant. It grows up out of the dirt. Sunlight and water help the sprout grow.

Corn plants grow tall.

Corn grows tall very fast. A **stalk** is the stem of a corn plant. A stalk can grow 5 inches (13 centimeters) in one day. It takes a girl or a boy two years to grow that much.

The farmer protects the plants.

Hungry bugs may eat the corn. Bugs can also give the corn diseases. Weeds may take up the corn's space. Weeds block out the sun too. Some farmers spray their crops to kill weeds and bugs.

Cobs grow.

Cobs grow on the corn stalks. Kernels grow on the cobs. Cobs with kernels are called **ears** of corn. Leaves cover each ear to protect it. These leaves are called **husks**.

The corn is picked.

Some farmers use a machine to pick the corn. Some farmers pick the corn by hand. This worker loads picked corn on a truck.

The corn is sold.

Many people buy fresh corn from a farmer's market or a grocery store. They take the corn home, take off the husks, and cook it.

Eat the corn!

Corn on the cob tastes good with butter, salt, and pepper. It tastes good all by itself!

Glossary

ears (EERZ): parts of a corn plant that grow seeds

husks (HUHSKS): leaves that cover an ear of corn

kernel (KUR-nuhl): a corn seed

root (ROOT): the part of a corn plant that grows under the ground

sprouts (SPROWTS): very young plants

stalk (STAWK): the stem of a corn plant